Science Discoveries

LOUIS

PASTEUR

and Germs

Steve Parker

Chelsea House Publishers
Philadelphia

First published in Great Britain in 1994 by
Belitha Press Limited, 31 Newington Green, London N16 9PU

5 7 9 8 6 4

Library of Congress Cataloging-in-Publication Data
Parker, Steve
    Louis Pasteur and germs/Steve Parker.
        p.   cm.—(Science discoveries)
    Includes bibliographical references and index.
    ISBN 0-7910-3002-4
    1. Pasteur, Louis, 1822-1895—Biography—Juvenile literature.
2. Science— History—Juvenile literature.   3. Medical sciences—
History—Juvenile literature.   4. Scientists—France—Biography—
Juvenile literature.   5. Medical scientists—France—Biography—
Juvenile literature.   [1. Pasteur, Louis, 1822-1895.   2. Scientists.]
I. Title.   II. Series: Science discoveries (1994)
Q143.P2P42   1994   94-8262
509.2—dc20   CIP
[B]   AC

Printed in Malaysia

Acknowledgements

Photographic credits:
Nick Birch 15 top left, 16 bottom
Bridgeman Art Library 19 bottom left Royal
    College of Surgeons, London
Mary Evans Picture Library 4 Town and Country
    Planning, 8 top and bottom, 10 bottom, 11 top,
    17 top, 19 center, 22 top, 24 bottom
Giraudon, Paris 14 top Chateau Versailles,
    25 bottom Lauros-Giraudon/Chateau
    Versailles, 26 Musée D'Orsay, Paris
Robert Harding Picture Library 27 bottom
    Alfred Wolf
Hulton Deutsch Collection 1, 10 top
Hutchison Library 20 Anna Tully
Mansell Collection 17 bottom, 23 top
Musée Pasteur, Institut Pasteur, Paris 5 all, 24 top,
    25 top

Retrograph Archive, London 16 top Martin Breese
Ann Ronan Picture Library/Image Select
    11 bottom, 15 bottom, 18 bottom, 19 top,
     23 bottom
Royal College of Physicians 19 bottom right
Science Photo Library 11 centre Dr. Jeremy
    Burgess, 12 Jean-Loup Charmet, 15 top right,
    18 top Dr. Rosalind King, 22 bottom CNRI,
    27 top right NIBSC, 27 top left Sinclair
    Stammers

Cover montage supplied by Mary Evans Picture
Library, Mansell Collection, Ann Ronan Picture
Library/Image Select

Illustrations: Peter Bull 9, 14, 20;
Tony Smith 6-7, 13, 21
Editor: Rachel Cooke
Designer: Andrew Oliver
Picture researcher: Juliet Duff
Specialist adviser: Dr Perry Williams

Contents

La Rue des Arènes in Dole, a quiet town on the graceful River Doubs, east of Dijon, France. Louis's parents settled here in about 1815.

Introduction

"Michelle had a sore throat, probably a **virus**. She stayed at home so that we couldn't catch it."

"Keep the flies off your food; they carry **germs**."

"Blow your nose into a paper tissue. Remember: coughs and sneezes spread diseases!"

Today, we are used to the idea that germs cause illnesses. We know how to kill germs and stop diseases spreading. Yet this knowledge is less than 150 years old. Before then, people had quite different ideas about how diseases were caused. Scientists used **microscopes**, but they did not appreciate the nature of the germs and other tiny living things they saw through them.

Louis Pasteur was a French chemist who was to change this. He founded the science of microbiology—the study of living things such as **bacteria** and viruses, which can be seen only with the aid of a microscope. His work made possible many important advances in medicine, public health, and hygiene. It has had immense effects on our daily lives, from the **vaccinations** that protect us against certain diseases to the safe milk we pour on our breakfast cereal each morning.

Chapter One
The Early Years

Louis Pasteur was born on December 27, 1822, in Dole, eastern France. His father owned a tannery, making and preparing leather. He had been in the army and won medals, and he had a tremendous pride in France and the achievements of his nation. Louis shared his father's national pride and kept it throughout his life.

When Louis was still a child, the family moved to Arbois, where he attended the local primary and secondary schools. Family life was uneventful, and Louis was an average pupil. His early interest was art. He drew pictures in chalks and charcoal and painted many portraits of his friends and family. At the age of 16, he was thinking about becoming a full-time artist. However, the principal at the college saw that Louis was a careful, willing student who thought clearly and logically. He advised the family that Louis should continue his education.

Louis was born in this humble house on the Rue des Tanneurs, Dole. In later life he attended a ceremony to unveil a plaque here, in his honor. The portraits of his parents (below) were painted by Louis himself.

The Pasteur house in Arbois, several miles southeast of Dole. Behind it were pits dug for the preparation of skins for tanning.

Pioneers in Chemistry

While Pasteur was a student and beginning his scientific career, several great scientists of the time inspired him in his work.

● Claude Bernard started the use of experiments in **physiology**. He studied the ways in which living things try to keep conditions inside their bodies constant, so that their bodily chemical reactions can work most effectively.

● Jean Baptiste Dumas was one of the founders of **organic chemistry** – the study of chemical processes involving carbon. (Most **molecules** in living things are based on carbon.) He studied, among other things, the chemistry of blood, muscles, and fats in animals.

● Justus Leibeg, the German chemist, worked out the chemical formulas for many organic substances. He also devised new ways of analyzing chemicals and pioneered the use of artificial fertilizers.

Colleges and Exams

In 1839, the young Pasteur went to the Royal College at Besançon. He passed his examinations to receive a Bachelor of Arts degree, then a Bachelor of Science degree. However, he was not very successful at the subject for which he would eventually become world famous. His chemistry examination was marked "mediocre."

Louis intended to continue his studies in the scientific classrooms of the famous École Normale Supérieure in Paris. But in 1842, he was placed 15th out of the 22 new students the École accepted. He thought this was not good enough, so delayed his move to the École Normale Supérieure. Instead he became a part-time student and teacher at a Paris boarding school, and attended courses at the Lycée Saint Louis. The next year, 1843, he began his course at the École Normale Supérieure, ranked fourth in the class. It was an early sign of his competitive personality.

During his student years, Pasteur worked hard and sometimes topped his class, especially in physics, chemistry, and mathematics. But he was not an outstanding student, merely "satisfactory." He gained his qualifications mainly by willpower and long hours of hard work. He received a Master of Science degree in 1845, and went on to an advanced degree in physical sciences. He obtained his Doctor of Science on August 23, 1847. He was making steady, if unspectacular, progress up the ladder of scientific qualifications.

Changing Plans

One of Pasteur's early influences was the well-known chemist Jean-Baptiste Dumas. Pasteur attended his lectures at the Sorbonne, along with 800 others—the lecture room was always full when Dumas spoke. Pasteur was impressed by Dumas's enthusiasm and careful preparation, his eloquence, and his way of making chemistry both exciting and mysterious. He remained a lifelong admirer of Dumas, and the two eventually became work colleagues and close friends.

Pasteur had always intended to teach and asked Dumas for a job as an assistant teacher. But soon his plans were changing. At the end of his time as a student at the École Normale Supérieure, his superiors said he "will make an excellent professor [teacher]." But Louis's thoughts were turning away from teaching as a profession, toward experiments and laboratories and the quest for new scientific knowledge.

A typical lecture scene during Pasteur's time as a student. He was so eager to enter the École Normale Supérieure that he arrived in Paris several days early and slept in the empty students' dormitory.

7

Chapter Two
A Brilliant Chemist

From about 1844-47, Louis Pasteur carried out his first important work in chemistry. He decided to investigate a puzzle involving tartrate **crystals**, obtained from **tartaric acid**, found in many fruits. German chemist Eilhard Mitscherlich had already shown that tartaric acid contained exactly the same chemical elements, in the same proportions, as another substance—**racemic (paratartaric) acid**. The puzzle was one difference between them. It involved a laboratory test using a special kind of light, called **polarized light**. When polarized light was shone through certain substances dissolved in water, it was rotated or "twisted." Tartaric acid rotated polarized light, but racemic acid did not. Why should this be?

Pasteur in 1865.

The École Normale Supérieure in Paris, where Pasteur was a student, and eventually administrator and director of scientific studies.

Mirror-Image Chemicals

Other chemists believed that crystals of tartaric acid and racemic acid were exactly the same shape. Pasteur guessed that he would find a tiny difference. He looked at them under the microscope. On close examination, racemic acid crystals were of two types. The slight difference between the types was in the arrangement of the flat faces, or **facets**. These were positioned exactly opposite to each other, like an object and its reflection in a mirror.

The crystals of tartaric acid, on the other hand, were all the same. In fact, they were identical to one of the racemic acid types.

Pasteur separated the two types of crystals by hand. One rotated polarized light to the left, and the other rotated it to the right. Racemic acid was a mixture of both types, so the lefts and rights canceled each other out. This was the reason why racemic acid did not affect polarized light, but tartaric acid did.

Today, it may not seem an earth-shattering piece of research. But this type of work was a vital part of the chemical investigations of the time, and Pasteur had scored a first-time success. He was so delighted with his achievement, he rushed out of the laboratory and embraced the first person he met. On May 22, 1848, Pasteur presented his report on the work to the Paris Academy of Sciences.

The Beginnings of Stereochemistry

Pasteur's early work on crystals led chemists to realize that the properties of substances depend not only on the ingredients or chemical elements in them, but also on the way these elements are positioned in relation to each other. This was reflected in their crystal shape. It was the beginning of **stereochemistry**, that is, the study of the arrangement in space of the various different elements in a substance and how this affects the substance's chemical behavior. This has become an important part of chemical analysis.

laevo-tartrate

dextro-tartrate

Two types of crystals of the salt of racemic acid. As you can see in the diagram, the crystals are very similar to each other. The difference is that laevo*-tartrate with the facet F on its left is an exact mirror image of the* dextro*-tartrate where F is on the right. Pasteur was the first to spot this.*

Marie Laurent (Madame Pasteur) with her husband in 1889.

The Chemistry Institute at Strasbourg, where Pasteur arrived on January 15, 1850.

Family Life

In 1849, Pasteur became a chemistry professor at a regional faculty (department) of the French university in Strasbourg. Here he met and, after a short court-ship, married Marie Laurent, the daughter of the rector at Strasbourg. They had five children: daughters Jeanne (1850), Cecile (1853), Marie-Louise (1858), and Camille (1863), and son Jean-Baptiste (1851). Only Jean-Baptiste and Marie-Louise survived to adulthood. Pasteur was deeply affected by the deaths of his young daughters, Jeanne in 1859 and Cecile in 1866, both from typhoid fever. This helped to spur him to his later research on human diseases.

Marie supported her husband in his work, taking notes and organizing his papers. He would complain that "the nights are too long," since the need for sleep kept him away from his beloved laboratory. Marie did not like Louis's long work hours. He once said to a colleague: "I am often scolded by Madame Pasteur [his wife], but I console her by telling her that I shall lead her to fame." Before he was 30 years old, Pasteur had developed an enormous faith that he would be a great scientist, like Galileo and Newton.

Wine is stored in barrels in order to mature. Wine making has long been a major French industry.

Researches in Fermentation

In 1854 Pasteur became dean and chemistry professor at the new Science Faculty in Lille. It was here, in the following year, that his keen interest in the chemistry of **fermentation** began. Among other things, fermentation describes the way sugary juices from grapes and other fruits bubble and turn into alcohol. The products, wine and beer, are part of French national tradition, and big money-makers.

It was French official policy to bring science to the service of industry and, in 1856, Pasteur received a query from Monsieur Bigo, head of one of the alcohol-making industries in Lille. His vats made alcohol from beet juice and other fruits and vegetables, but the products kept souring or spoiling (going bad). Could Pasteur, the well-known chemist, help?

The rounded single cells of wine yeasts, responsible for fermenting wine, magnified about 1,000 times.

At the time, most eminent scientists believed that fermentation was simply a **chemical reaction**. Tiny blobs had been seen in fermenting mixtures under the microscope, but these blobs – which are living things called yeasts – were thought to be unimportant and probably not even alive.

One of Pasteur's early designs for equipment to cool and ferment beer. The candle and spy hole allow viewing of the contents.

Microbes

- **Microbes** and **micro-organisms** are living things that can be seen only with the aid of a microscope. Most microbes are less than one-tenth of a millimeter long, and most consist of only one **cell**.
- **Bacteria** are one main group of microbes, which Pasteur and his colleagues saw under the microscope. They live almost everywhere, in water and soil and in other living things. Some bacteria are harmful, causing diseases. Others are helpful, for example, those that live in the gut and take part in the normal process of digestion.
- **Yeasts** are microbes which belong to the **fungus** group, which also includes mushrooms and toadstools. Much of Pasteur's work was on yeasts in wines and beers.
- **Germs** are now thought of as microbes that cause harm. So some bacteria are germs. The word germ was originally used to describe a seed of life, that is, life at its very beginning. The word in this sense is still used in the term "wheat germ."

Pasteur developed a theory that the tiny blobs were alive. They were yeast **microbes**, and as they lived, they turned sugar into alcohol. This was received with amusement, even horror, by some great scientists of the day. They made fun of Pasteur, asking whether his microbes were tiny animals that ate sugar, bubbled **carbon dioxide** gas out of their backsides, and expelled alcohol like we expel urine!

However, Pasteur went on to design careful experiments for testing his theory. He showed that fermentation did not happen unless the tiny blobs of living yeasts were present. If other microbes were present in the sugary juice, such as rod-shaped bacteria, then the fermentation was spoiled. The sugar turned not into alcohol, but **lactic acid**. This demonstrated that microbes could play a vital part in chemical changes. The science of microbiology was founded.

In 1856 Pasteur published his findings. The alcohol-making industries followed his advice about arranging conditions and preventing contamination of their vats. They were very grateful as their profits rose.

Pasteur "discovers the law of fermentation." He showed that microbes are responsible for spoiling the wine.

Edité par la CHOCOLATERIE D'AIGUEBELLE (Monastère de la Trappe-Drôme)

PASTEUR DÉCOUVRE LA LOI DES FERMENTS

Chapter Three
The Discovery of Germs

In *Mémoire sur la fermentation appelée lactique* ("Report on Lactic Fermentation") published in 1858 and based on his work in Lille, Pasteur suggested that different microbes caused different types of fermentation—and that microbes might also cause various diseases. This was a foundation for the **germ theory of disease**, developed over many years.

By this time, Pasteur had returned to Paris. He became administrator and director of scientific studies at his old college, the École Normale Supérieure. He continued the study of yeasts and fermentation. His laboratory was a small attic room, and his incubator for growing microbes in warmth was a cupboard under the stairs! But his skills at practical work overcame these limitations.

Pasteur was now a very ambitious man, confident, and ready to take on challenges and argue in public with his competitors. Colleagues spoke of his strong personality and enthusiasm, which inspired his friends but which also made enemies.

Pasteur's attic laboratory at the École Normale Supérieure, in about 1858.

Napoleon III, French emperor from 1852 to 1870.

Killing Germs With Heat

During the mid-1860s, Pasteur made one of his greatest discoveries. In 1863 he was asked by Napoleon III, the ruler of France's Second Empire, to help the French wine makers. They were losing vast amounts of money because after fermentation, the wines kept turning sour. He discovered that contaminating microbes in the wine caused this souring – and that they could be destroyed by heat. The idea was extended to other perishable foods and drinks. These could be preserved by careful heating to kill any harmful microbes they contained.

Pasteur developed the process now named after him, **pasteurization** (see figure). The wine makers were suspicious of the "small bearded professor with the microscope," but they soon took up the process when its success was revealed.

Pasteurization

This process uses heat to kill off microbes in foods and drink, which would otherwise multiply and spoil them. Carried out correctly, it should have little effect on appearance or taste.

In the 1860s, Pasteur showed that heating wine or beer above 135°F (57°C) would kill any germs in it. This meant the wine and beer would keep much longer without going bad.

Today, milk and many milk and egg products, are pasteurized. A modern HTST (high temperature, short time) pasteurizing machine heats milk to 130°F (72°C) for 15 seconds, then cools it to below 18°F (10°C).

Milk Pasteurization

pasteurization by heating

cooled storage tank

separation into skimmed milk and cream

skimmed milk storage

milk and cream remixed

cream storage

bottling of milk into sterilized bottles

This microscope was used by Pasteur himself. The engraving of Aspergillus *fungus is from his book on the studies of beer (see page 16).*

Life From Nothing?

At this time, Pasteur became concerned with the notion of **spontaneous generation** (see figure), which maintained life could appear from nonliving matter. His experiments showed that "clean air" contained floating microbes, **spores** and other living things. These could be trapped in **asbestos** filters and grown on special **nutrient** substances called **culture media** in laboratory equipment.

Pasteur also tested nutrient liquids, which would normally go bad through bacterial action. He showed they remained unchanged, even for months, if they were first sterilized by heat and then kept in glass vessels with "swan necks" or special seals. The swan necks allowed in the oxygen necessary for life, but kept out microbe-bearing dust particles. No life appeared.

On April 7, 1864, at the Sorbonne, Pasteur used the results of his experiments to argue against spontaneous generation. Referring to the still-clear liquid, in which life had not spontaneously appeared, Pasteur said: "I have kept from it the only thing man cannot produce . . . the germs which float in the air."

A swan-necked flask like that Pasteur used in his studies of spontaneous generation.

Spontaneous Generation

The idea of spontaneous generation was that under certain conditions, life could appear from simple non-living ingredients. It had developed in ancient times, to describe how maggots appeared in meat and meal-worms in grain stores.

Gradually, experiments showed that creatures such as maggots hatched from tiny eggs laid by flies. By Pasteur's time no one believed in spontaneous generation of this kind. But some believed that microbes appeared spontaneously in nutrient-rich broth. Pasteur helped to show that the unseen microbes in the air floated onto the broth.

Today, many scientists accept a modified version of the theory of spontaneous generation. Modern views on **evolution** imply that the first simple life forms appeared from nonliving substances at a very early stage in the Earth's history. This explains the origin of life itself.

Rewards—and Disaster

In 1867 Napoleon III created a laboratory of physical chemistry for Pasteur at the École Normale Supérieure. It was a great honor for the chemist, who always had tremendous national pride. At this time, he took up the post of chemistry professor at the Sorbonne, the University of Paris, but continued to work in his new laboratory at the École Normale.

Then at the age of 45, on October 19, 1868, he suffered a stroke. This gradually paralyzed the left side of his body. However, he still continued his work.

The huge wine vats and bottling equipment at a French vineyard, in about 1880. Pasteur's research helped reduce wastage in wine production.

Modern pasteurization vessels process hundreds of quarts of milk or other liquids every second.

Helping French Industries

In 1876 Pasteur published *Études sur la bière, ses maladies, et causes qui les provoquent* ("Studies on Beer, Its Diseases, and the Causes That Provoke Them"). This described how some microbes, unlike the vast majority of living things, did not need **oxygen** to live. Indeed, they perished if oxygen was present. Pasteur had discovered what we now call **anaerobic microbes**, which cause living matter to rot.

His work on fermentation and preservation had enormous benefits to the French food and drink industries. Through improvements in beer and wine production, vast amounts of money were saved.

Chapter Four
Preventing Disease

During his research into fermentation, Louis Pasteur was also active in other areas of science. Foremost was his study of disease, first in animals, then in humans.

The Curse of Anthrax

Anthrax is a serious illness caused by the germ *Bacillus anthracis.* In Pasteur's day it affected many cattle, sheep, horses, goats, and similar animals, often causing death. People who worked closely with these animals or handled their products such as skins and wool, were also at risk from it. They suffered sore, swollen areas on the body, fever, in some cases pneumonia, blood poisoning, and the risk of death.

In 1876 the German scientist Robert Koch discovered that the germs responsible for anthrax could be grown in the laboratory. Koch was a general physician in Prussia, who built upon much of Pasteur's work on germ theory. Koch showed that certain bacteria were responsible for particular diseases, and he identified, named, and grouped them.

Robert Koch at work. He received a Nobel prize for his work on bacteria in 1905.

The rod-shaped Bacillus anthracis *bacteria responsible for anthrax, magnified about 500 times. They have been stained with a laboratory dye to make them easier to see.*

In the meantime, Pasteur suggested that the spread of anthrax could be reduced by burning the bodies of its animal victims rather than burying them or leaving them to rot. His experiments showed that resistant spores of the anthrax bacteria stayed in the soil, spread by earthworms and windblown dust, for many years.

The Road to Vaccination

In 1880, summer holidays delayed one of Pasteur's experiments on a disease known as **fowl cholera**, which affected chickens. His assistant Charles Chamberland forgot to inject some chickens with germs, and did so when he returned after the break. Strangely, the birds did not die. They became ill, but then recovered.

Pasteur devised a theory. The cholera-causing germs had been weakened, or attenuated, probably by exposure to air through the summer holidays. Then thinking of the work of Edward Jenner (see panel) he injected the same hens with fresh cholera germs. They survived. Another group of birds, new from the market, died when injected with the fresh cholera germs. Somehow the earlier dose of weakened germs made the first batch of chickens resistant to the disease.

This work was immensely significant. It paved the way for the process of vaccination and **immunization**.

Following the work of Pasteur and his colleagues, vaccination soon became established and even fashionable. This illustration shows free vaccination against smallpox using the fluid from cowpox sores on the premises of a French magazine in 1905.

Sheep being vaccinated against anthrax, in about 1882. Pasteur's work helped to save the lives of thousands of farm animals.

In 1881, Pasteur and his co-workers developed further methods for weakening germs, in this case, the bacteria of anthrax. In a famous experiment in May, a group of 25 sheep were given the weakened anthrax germs; another group of 25, kept in the same conditions, were not. Later all the sheep were given the full-strength anthrax bacteria. All those which had received the weakened bacteria survived. Nearly all the others died from anthrax. This was the first use of artificially-weakened germs, in a vaccine, to give protection against the same disease later. Pasteur and his team had no idea how the protection, which we now call immunity, developed. But they reasoned that it could save human lives.

Initially, fun was made of Jenner's ideas. People claimed that those receiving his vaccine would become part cow!

In Honor of Jenner

In about 1796, English physician Edward Jenner had developed a method of protecting people against smallpox. He gave them a weaker form of the illness, called cowpox or *vaccinia*, which usually affected cattle and people who worked with them. After developing mild cowpox, these people were resistant to the much more serious smallpox.

Pasteur suggested that the term vaccination should be extended to cover any process using weakened germs to make the body resistant – immune – to the full-strength ones.

The hand with cowpox sores from which Jenner made his first smallpox vaccine.

Edward Jenner (1749-1823)

The Process of Immunization

The germs that cause a disease are isolated.

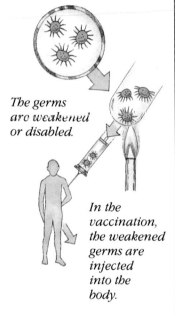

The germs are weakened or disabled.

In the vaccination, the weakened germs are injected into the body.

The body's immune processes destroy the weakened germs.

The body can now destroy even the full-strength germs.

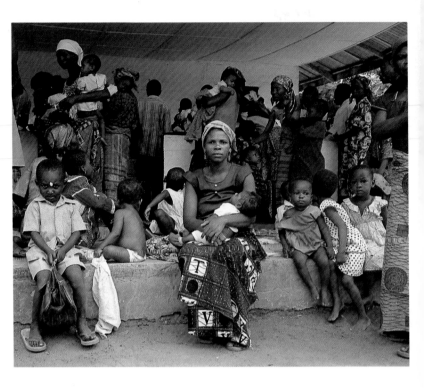

People wait for vaccinations in Nigeria. Large-scale vaccination offers the best hope of conquering many major infectious diseases.

Vaccination and Immunity

The work of Edward Jenner and Louis Pasteur has led directly to the lifesaving immunizations of today. In the process of vaccination, you are given an injection or preparation of specially weakened or disabled germs. You only suffer very slightly, if at all, from the disease. But your body reacts as though the germs are normal, full-strength ones. It develops ways of killing these particular germs quickly. Next time they appear, even if they are full strength, they are soon inactivated. You are unlikely to catch the disease. This is called immunity.

Today, we are usually vaccinated during childhood against diseases such as diphtheria, tetanus, pertussis (whooping cough), polio, measles, mumps, and rubella (German measles), and possibly tuberculosis.

Chapter Five
Reducing Human Suffering

Medicine in Pasteur's time had its dangers. Some treatments were more likely to kill patients than cure them. However, through the 19th century, doctors and scientists made steady progress in reducing the risks.

In 1847, Hungarian doctor Ignaz Semmelweiss reduced the spread of childbed (puerperal) fever, which affected many women with new babies. He suggested that before attending a new birth, the doctor should wash his hands! It may seem obvious today, because now it is always done; but at the time, doctors did not understand about germs and infection.

By 1865, British surgeon Joseph Lister was the first to use **carbolic acid (phenol)** on wounds during surgery. The carbolic acid acted as an **antiseptic**, or germ killer. It prevented the wounds from becoming infected by germs from the air or on the hands and instruments of the surgeons. This quickly reduced the death rate after operations. Lister derived his ideas on antiseptics partly from Pasteur's work on microbes in the air.

In 1871, France lost the Franco-Prussian War. (Prussia is now part of Germany.) The French surgeons in the army hospitals were urged to adopt the practices of Lister by sterilizing their instruments and their patients' wounds. Despite this, only 3,000 patients survived of the 13,000 who had surgery! Over the next 50 years this type of statistic was to improve dramatically.

Surgeons use the "Lister spray" of carbolic acid (phenol), in about 1882.

The Mystery Germs

The germ theory was so successful that it was used to explain diseases like measles and rabies that spread as though they were caused by microbes—but no one could find them. It was suggested that the microbes were too small to be seen under the microscopes of the time and too small even to be trapped by special chemical filters. These theoretical microbes were called "filterable viruses." For many years after Pasteur, they were studied by their effects on laboratory chemicals and living things. Not until the invention of the more powerful **electron microscopes** in this century, could people see viruses directly.

An artificially-colored electron microscope view of a single virus. This is the type of virus that causes influenza (flu), magnified 200,000 times.

The Germ Theory of Disease

Pasteur made sense of these medical advances, and encouraged a fuller understanding of illness, through the germ theory of disease. In 1878 he published *La théorie des germes et ses applications à la médicine et la chirurgie* ("The Germ Theory and Its Application to Medicine and Surgery").

The germ theory states that certain diseases are caused by germs. These get into, or infect, the body. If not neutralized by the body's defense system, they multiply and cause illness. Each disease is caused by a different type of germ. In Pasteur's time, these proposals were a tremendous breakthrough in the understanding of illness.

The theory was first applied to bacteria, but it was soon being extended to cover other types of microbes, such as **protozoa** and fungi.

In 1882, Robert Koch found the cause of the widespread and deadly tuberculosis (TB). It was a bacterial germ, duly named *Mycobacterium tuberculosis*. This was the first definite link between a germ and a human disease. Soon the laboratories of Pasteur, Koch, and others developed vaccines against diseases such as cholera, tuberculosis, tetanus, and diphtheria.

Research into Rabies

In 1882 Pasteur and his assistants tried to find the microbe which they assumed was the cause of rabies. They thought it was present in the saliva (spit) of infected dogs, and that it was spread by bites. But they could not see the germ under the microscope.

Their research showed that the rabies "agent" was also present in dogs' brains and nerves. They discovered that, like other germs, it could be weakened – in this case, by drying the nerve tissue. This suggested a way of producing an antirabies vaccine.

On July 6, 1885, after successful experiments with the antirabies vaccine in dogs, Pasteur tried it on a human. A young boy, Joseph Meister, had been bitten 14 times by a rabid dog. His mother pleaded with Pasteur to save him. It was a terrible decision. Had the boy caught rabies from the bites? If not, might the vaccine actually *give* him rabies? Pasteur decided to proceed.

Sixty hours after the bites, Joseph received the first of 12 antirabies injections. The vaccines were made from the spinal nerves of rabbits. The boy survived. A vaccine of the type developed by Pasteur is still used today. It is given to people who may have been infected, but only before they show signs of the disease. Once someone becomes ill with rabies, showing the virus has gained hold, death is the usual outcome.

The "Mad Dog" Disease

Rabies is dangerous and frightening. It affects animals such as dogs, cats, foxes, skunks, and racoons, as well as people. People may catch the virus after being bitten by an infected animal. The disease affects the brain and nerves. About 10-50 days after being infected, the person becomes depressed and restless, then very excitable with fever, muscle spasms, convulsions, extra salivation, and paralysis. He or she becomes very thirsty but cannot drink because of the throat spasms. This led to another name for the illness, hydrophobia, meaning "fear of water."

The picture above shows one of the dogs to which Pasteur gave his antirabies vaccine.

Pasteur watches as an assistant vaccinates Joseph Meister.

Chapter Six
The Later Years

Pasteur and his family in the garden at Arbois, 1892.

True to his belief in the greatness of France, Pasteur's scientific achievements brought many benefits to his nation. The chemist-turned-microbiologist was now a world figure. He traveled to the Congress of Hygiene in 1882 in Geneva to report on ways of weakening viruses. Two years later, despite his continuing paralysis, he spoke before the International Congress of Medicine in Copenhagen on vaccines for harmful microbes.

Controversies over Rabies

In 1888 Pasteur became the first director of the new *Institut Pasteur,* the Pasteur Institute, in Paris. It had been funded by international donations and by government grants in gratitude for his work, but there had been problems. Pasteur's view of rabies and its vaccine had been challenged by scientists, governments, and the public alike. How did he know the vaccinated people were infected with rabies in the first place? The suspected rabies germs were too small to be detected, and many people bitten by mad dogs never developed rabies.

There was also opposition from people who were against experiments on animals because of the way the rabies virus was grown in live rabbits.

During 1888, Pasteur would spend his afternoons watching the building of the Pasteur Institute.

Final Honors

Pasteur's work to support his views was exhausting and took its toll on him. The year of 1892 was celebrated by a "Pasteur Jubilee" at the Sorbonne in Paris on his 70th birthday. His memory and health were now failing, due to a second attack of paralysis in 1887. During the summer of 1894 he visited the family home at Arbois for the final time. He was still director of the Pasteur Institute when he died on September 28, 1895. He was greatly honored at his funeral and buried in a tomb within the building.

The funeral of Louis Pasteur held in great state at the Palace of Versailles.

Chapter Seven
Pasteur in Perspective

The momentous achievements for which Louis Pasteur is remembered are not confined to one scientific area. He was a founder of stereochemistry, with his work on tartaric acid, and of microbiology. His proposal that diseases are caused by germs was one of the most important in the history of medicine, and it is a foundation of modern medical thinking. When a new illness is discovered that seems to be transferred from person to person, such as Legionnaire's disease or AIDS, researchers at once look for the causative germs.

Pasteur was a tireless experimenter. He spent many long hours in the laboratory carrying out chemical processes, looking down the microscope, and making notes. He had great powers of concentration.

The electron micro-scope (left) sees much smaller objects than the microscopes of Pasteur's time, such as a human blood cell magnified 2,000 times (below). The green dots are HIVs, the viruses that cause AIDS.

Preserving Food and Drink

Pasteur's work on fermentation advanced the understanding of how beer, wine, bread, and other foodstuffs are made. He showed how procedures could be devised to keep food and drink from spoiling or going bad. This has saved vast amounts of money for the food and drink industries, and innumerable cases of illness for consumers.

Building on the work of Jenner, Pasteur and his colleagues made possible the process of vaccination, which has doubtless saved millions of lives through the years. Over the last century, diseases such as cholera, tuberculosis, and rubella have become easy to prevent, while smallpox has been eradicated.

In 1967 the World Health Organization began a campaign of mass vaccination and treatment against smallpox. The numbers of sufferers gradually went down. At last, in 1979 the world was declared "smallpox free." There are still some smallpox viruses—but they are locked in research laboratories. Through the work of Pasteur and others, many more diseases may be similarly controlled.

A World Center for Science

At first, the main work of the Pasteur Institute was research and treatment of rabies, following methods established by Pasteur himself. The Institute soon became a world center not only for research into the prevention and treatment of diseases but also for the production of vaccines and for work in general micro-biology. It is still based in Paris, and it is closely associated with the Pasteur Hospital there. The Institute and Hospital are fitting tributes for a man who made enormous advances in many areas of science and who did so much to ease the burden of human suffering.

A scientist wearing protective mask and gloves, at work at the Pasteur Institute, Paris.

The World in Pasteur's Time

	1800-1825	**1826-1850**
Science	**1804** Richard Trevithick builds an early type of steam locomotive **1821** Michael Faraday demonstrates the principle of the electric motor **1822** Louis Pasteur is born	**1826** Joseph Niépce takes the first photograph on a metal plate **1831** Charles Darwin sets sail on his voyage around the world in the *Beagle*
Exploration	**1803** The first European settlers arrive in Tasmania **1818** John Ross and other expeditions fail to find the Northwest Passage, following a handsome reward offered by George III of England	**1831** James Ross discovers the magnetic North Pole **1837** Beer and Madler make the first accurate map of the Moon **1847** The first reports of gorillas reach Europe from Africa
Politics	**1815** Napoleon's French army is defeated by Wellington at the Battle of Waterloo **1821** Mexico and Peru declare independence from Spain	**1833** British parliament abolishes slavery **1848** The July revolution topples Louis Philippe, France's last king, and establishes the Second Republic
Art	**1814** Franz Schubert completes his first opera at the age of 17 **1816** Jane Austen writes *Emma* **1820** *Venus de Milo* statue, over 2,000 years old, is discovered on the Greek island of Melos	**1843** The tuba becomes a regular member of the orchestra **1844-5** Alexandre Dumas finishes writing *The Three Musketeers* and *The Count of Monte Cristo*

1851-1875	1876-1900

1861 The first daily weather forecasts are issued in Britain

1862 Richard Gatling patents his machine gun

1869 Dmitri Mendeleev publishes the first version of the periodic table of chemical elements

1853 David Livingstone discovers the Victoria Falls of the Zambezi river

1869 American Union Pacific Railway crosses the continent

1857 The Indian Mutiny fails to throw off British rule

1864 Jean Dunant founds the International Red Cross in Switzerland

1871 France is defeated in the Franco-Prussian War

1853 Richard Wagner begins to compose *The Ring of the Nibelung*, a cycle of four operas, that takes him over 20 years to complete

1872 Claude Monet paints *Impression: Sunrise*, and the school of painting known as Impressionism is named from it

1877 Thomas Edison invents first versions of the gramophone

1880 The protozoa that cause malaria are found to be carried by certain kinds of mosquito

1895 Louis Pasteur dies

1877 Astronomers see and map the "canals" of Mars

1884 Greenwich Mean Time becomes the basis of the world time zones

1883 The island of Krakatoa, Southeast Asia, disappears in a huge volcanic eruption

1876 General Custer makes his last stand against the Sioux at the Battle of Little Bighorn

1879 Europeans finally defeat the Zulus in South Africa

1886 Auguste Rodin finishes his sculpture *The Kiss*

1888 Vincent Van Gogh paints his famous series of sunflower paintings

1890 Henrik Ibsen's play *Hedda Gabler* is first performed

Glossary

anaerobic microbes: microscopic living things that do not need *oxygen* to survive and even die in its presence, unlike all other living things.

anthrax: a disease that affects mainly farm animals and sometimes people, caused by *bacteria*. Among its effects are sore, raw areas of skin and severe chest problems.

antiseptic: a chemical used to kill or disable germs.

asbestos: a type of mineral fiber, usually containing chemicals known as silicates. It has uses in laboratory and chemical processes, insulation, and fireproofing.

bacteria (singular **bacterium**): a group of *microbes* which live almost everywhere. There are many thousands of different kinds. Some are harmful and cause diseases.

carbolic acid (phenol): a chemical with the formula C_6H_5OH, which is usually in the form of white *crystals* that can dissolve in water. Carbolic acid was one of the first *antiseptics* and is still used as a germ killer.

carbon dioxide: one of the gases in the air. It is colorless with hardly any smell. It is given out by living things, from *yeasts* to humans, and when anything containing carbon burns.

cell: the smallest unit of life, or part of a living thing, only visible under a *microscope*. Some living things are just one cell, like *bacteria* and *yeasts*. The human body is made of millions upon millions of different cells.

chemical reaction: when two or more substances combine or interact together in some way to form different products. An example is coal (carbon, C) reacting with *oxygen* (O_2) to form *carbon dioxide* (CO_2) in the chemical reaction we call burning.

crystal: a solid substance with a regular shape or form with flat sides and sharp edges and corners. Different substances have crystals of different shapes and colors.

culture media: substances for growing *microbes,* usually watery or jellylike, used in laboratories and factories. They contain all the *nutrients* that the microbes need to multiply.

electron microscope: a very powerful *microscope* that uses beams of particles called electrons rather than light. It can see in more detail than a light microscope.

evolution: changes with time, especially in animals, plants, and other living things.

facets: the faces or flat surfaces on a crystal.

fermentation: the breaking down of certain substances into others caused by the action of microbes. Among other things, we use fermentation to make wine, beer, and breads.

fowl cholera: a severe digestive infection caused by a *bacteria* that affects fowl (chickens and similar birds).

fungus (plural **fungi**): a member of one of the main groups, or kingdoms, of living things. In the past, fungi have been grouped with plants but now they are usually put in a group of their own. Unlike plants, they feed by breaking down or rotting other living things. Mushrooms, toadstools, mildews, rusts, and yeasts are all fungi.

germ: any microbe that causes disease.

germ theory of disease: the proposal that, for the group of diseases called infections, each type of disease is caused by a certain type of germ. For example, tuberculosis is caused by the tuberculosis bacterium *Mycobacterium tuberculosis.*

immunization: the process of becoming immune, or resistant, to a disease – see *vaccination*. When immune, the body has the ability to quickly kill the microbes that cause the disease.

lactic acid: a substance with the chemical formula $C_3H_6O_3$, also known as 2-hydroxypropanic acid. It is made by the *fermentation* processes of some *bacteria* and also in muscles when they are very active.

microbe or **microorganism:** a living thing that is so small it can only be seen under the microscope.

microscope: a device that magnifies very small things, making them look hundreds or thousands of times bigger than they really are.

molecule: the smallest particle of a substance that can exist by itself and still have all the chemical properties of that substance.

nutrient: food, or the substances a living thing needs to survive and grow.

organic chemistry: the study of compounds that contain carbon. Carbon compounds are found in all living *cells*.

oxygen: a colorless gas with no smell that makes up about one-fifth of the air around us. The vast majority of living things need oxygen in order to survive.

pasteurization: treating milk and similar substances with heat to destroy harmful microbes.

pebrine: a disease of silkworms, the caterpillars of the silkworm moth, caused by the *protozoa* named *Nosema bombycis*. Tiny dark spots grow on and in the caterpillars' bodies, and they usually die before spinning their silken cocoons.

physiology: the scientific study of the processes of life in animals and plants.

polarized light: light in which the up-and-down motions of the light waves are all parallel or traveling in the same direction. Light waves usually form a random pattern.

protozoa: a group of *microbes*. They are single-celled animals.

racemic (paratartaric) acid: a mixture of the two forms of *tartaric acid*.

spontaneous generation: when living things appear to develop from nonliving substances.

spores: microscopic structures produced by certain living things, such as bacteria and fungi. Under the right conditions, they grow into new versions of their parent.

stereochemistry: the study of the arrangement of the different elements in a substance and how this affects the substance's chemical behavior.

tartaric acid: a crystal substance with the chemical formula $C_4H_6O_6$. It is formed in grapes and other fruits. It occurs in two forms. The *dextro*-tartaric acid bends *polarized light* to the right; the mirror-image crystal *laevo*-tartaric acid bends it to the left.

vaccination: the technique of giving a person (or other living thing) weakened forms of a germ, such as a bacteria, to bring about *immunization*.

virus: minute things that cause some diseases. They are smaller than *bacteria* and other *microbes* and can only be seen with an *electron microscope*. All viruses are harmful because they can only multiply by taking over and destroying the cells of living things.

yeasts: microscopic, bloblike *fungi*, each consisting of a single *cell*. Some types of yeasts are useful, being involved in *fermentation*.

Index

STEVE PARKER has written more than 40 books for children, including
several volumes in the Eyewitness series. He has a bachelor of science degree
in zoology and is a member of the Zoological Society of London.